Poetry and Science: Writing Our Way to Discovery is a timely and fascinating exploration of how science plays into the making of poetry and therefore the larger making (and to a degree, unmaking) of our world. But it's much more than that, too. As Allison Adelle Hedge Coke writes, "Poets and scientists share a main line—curiosity. It inspires and activates us wholly." And so more than an examination of how science informs poetry, this unique collection of essays and poetry from a wonderful selection of today's best science-smart poets—Alison Hawthorne Deming, Ann Fisher-Wirth, Elizabeth Bradfield, Allison Adelle Hedge Coke, and Lucille Lang Day— provides keen insight into the framework of our rapidly changing world, both literary and technical. It asks: What role do poetry and science play in solving the grand challenges facing humanity today? It answers, to quote Ann Fisher-Worth: "We are one." Or Elizabeth Bradfield: "I seek to be attuned. Attending is all." If attending is all, then where *Poetry and Science* particularly delights is in the personal nature of the pieces—how the poet-scientists and scientist-poets came to love science and poetry, how they are created by that broad mix and likewise help to further the discourse between and beyond the two. These are not, thankfully, just academic papers. They are, rather, personal essays supported by place- and science-rich poetry—they come from origin stories and conclude in what Alison Hawthorne Deming calls "applied poetics." They are captivating, masterful, essential.

—Simmons Buntin, Editor-in-Chief of *Terrain.org*
Coeditor of *Dear America: Letters of Hope, Habitat, Defiance, and Democracy*
Author of *Bloom, Riverfall*, and *Unsprawl: Remixing Spaces as Places*

POETRY
& SCIENCE
WRITING OUR WAY TO DISCOVERY

edited by LUCILLE LANG DAY

BOOKS
Oakland, California

❧

Front cover art by Barbara Rogers
"Desert Night Pond #1," 2016
Oil encaustic and plant materials on panel
8"x10" www.barbararogersart.com

Cover & interior book design by Fred Dodsworth

❧

Published by Scarlet Tanager Books
P.O. Box 20906
Oakland, CA 94620
www.scarlettanager.com

ISBN 978-1-7345313-3-6
Library of Congress Control Number: 2021938751

CONTENTS

POETRY & SCIENCE

WRITING OUR WAY TO DISCOVERY

"Science arose from poetry, and…when times change, the two can meet again on a higher level as friends."

— Johann Wolfgang von Goethe

"Dogma and shrinking from the external world are at one limit of the range of belief. At the other are science and poetry and, indeed, reality."

— Muriel Rukeyser

PREFACE

MY ENTHUSIASM for poetry and science began early: my first heroes were Emily Dickinson, whose poem "Success is counted sweetest" appeared in my fifth-grade reader, and Madame Curie, whose biography I read when I was seventeen. As a young adult, I revered Sylvia Plath and Rachel Carson equally, and I did not perceive any contradiction in believing in the power of both poetry and science, nor did I think of science as a field more congenial to the male psyche than the female one.

Since then, I've learned that all human cultures have poetry, and that Enheduanna, the first known author to sign her work, was a poet. This was in about 2300 BCE. The origins of modern science don't appear in the human record, though, until almost 2,000 years later, in the fifth century BCE in Greece. It seems significant to me that poetry came before science. Perhaps this means that poetry comes more easily than science to the human brain and can therefore be used as a vehicle to help us understand science.

But that's not all: as I continued reading about poetry and science, I learned that poets can make intuitive leaps, or pre-discoveries, that are later confirmed by science. Edgar Allan Poe predicted black holes, the expanding universe, and the Big Bang long before scientists thought of these things. He was also the first person to figure out that the sky is dark at night because the universe is finite. He did not write scientific papers about any of these things: he described them in *Eureka: A Prose Poem*, which was first published in 1848. Walt Whitman also made a pre-discovery. Going against the scientific teachings of his time, he argued that mind depends upon flesh. Gertrude Stein not only found a new way to write poetry but simultaneously showed that the brain's neural structures for grammar are independent of the meaning of words. She was way ahead of the linguists!

The history of poetry and science confirms my initial, intuitive conviction that these are not totally separate endeavors. This excites me greatly, and in *Poetry and Science: Writing Our Way to Discovery*, I wanted to bring together four of my favorite poets who use science extensively in their work: Alison Hawthorne Deming, Ann Fisher-Wirth, Elizabeth Bradfield, and Allison Adelle Hedge Coke. It is no coincidence that they are women, as women have often wrested science from its own biases (historically white, straight, and male) to dynamic complications. I hope you will enjoy their thoughts on poetry, science, and discovery as much as I do. It was an honor to collaborate with them on this book.

Lucille Lang Day
Oakland, California, July 2021

Alison Hawthorne Deming

POETRY AND SCIENCE: THE BIG STORY

IN MY CHILDHOOD, books brought me joy, new knowledge, corroboration of my fears, the redemptive power of love, and an introduction to astonishment. My books were not only literature (such as *Stuart Little, Pinocchio*, my mother's original illustrated edition of *The Wizard of Oz*, and the remarkable feminist fable by Wanda Gág, *Gone Is Gone*). I also had pocket-sized guides to trees and wildflowers, editions that still grace my bookshelves. I am delighted to note that my copy of *Trees You Want to Know*, by Donald Culross Peattie, is marked with my first attempts to write my name (pretty good except that the capital "N" is flipped backward). I also had a children's natural history encyclopedia, perhaps purchased on a family trip to the American Museum of Natural History in New York City, an experience that certainly shaped my religious feelings as a child growing up in a secular family—religious in the sense of awe inspiring, of feeling that I belonged to something mysterious that stirred in me a reverence. Dinosaurs, those monstrous and beautiful beings that stood at the evolutionary portal of my very existence, were among the childhood gods of my godless childhood. I spent hours in daydream gazing at their images on those pages. Literature included art and science for me. These were not disciplines but windows into the larger world.

In a high school biology class, my teacher drew a diagram on the greenboard to illustrate a time in deep history when science and religion took separate paths as ways of understanding that larger world and our place in it. I realized that science had been a source of wonder and discovery for me since early childhood. That in some strange way it had been my religion, leading me to feel a part of something more vast than human life. And that the detail with which science investigated the world was a great, continuously unfolding story. I did not realize for another few decades that poetry would become the road I'd travel, and that science would challenge me to rethink the language and form of what I might consider poetic.

From early on I had an epistemological sense of what poetry was for: How do we know what we know? What are the forms of knowledge that I yearn for? That I trust? I found that I could not separate poetry from science, particularly natural history, as a field of inquiry into how I came to be the creature I am or for understanding what the Alaska poet John Haines described as "the terms of my existence." Nothing was more interesting to me than the Big Story of Life on Earth. Nothing more soul crushing than the diminishment of life on Earth at the hands of human cruelty and greed.

The title poem of my first book, *Science and Other Poems*, began what has become a practice of being, as one colleague dubbed me, a lay scientist. I am not trained as a scientist, but I am inspired by science and read widely in various fields, as certain projects prescribe. This interest has acquired urgency as the denigration, suppression, and denial of science have rabidly spread in the last several decades, a time during which science literacy is essential to solving our most weighty challenges, including climate change, health care, environmental justice.

So, given those concerns in which facts are essential, the poet faces the challenges of (1) transforming information into images; (2) finding patterns in nature that suggest an approach to form; (3) getting beyond the outrage and elegy that are the dominant emotional hue of our discontent ("We must not let our grief rob us of our joy in nature," as I heard Bill McKibben urge after one of his depressing *End of Nature* talks); (4) taking on complexity without sacrificing clarity (Ross Gay's *Catalog of Unabashed Gratitude*, A. R. Ammons's *Garbage*); and (5) exploring the limits of scientific diction in poetic discourse (Kimiko Hahn's *Toxic Flora*).

My second book of poems, *The Monarchs: A Poem Sequence*, began when I moved to California for a Stegner Fellowship at Stanford in 1987. While there I had the opportunity to attend a conference on consciousness that featured neuroscientists and research psychologists and such. I was jazzed by the concepts but found the language stultifying, what an evolutionary biologist once described to me as "journal-induced narcolepsy." During that time in California, I was also encountering a natural world that was alien to me as a tenth-generation New Englander. Grass turning green in January? Species I knew as diminutive houseplants showing up as treelike versions of themselves in people's yards? Most awesome and unsettling of all were the hundreds of thousands of monarch butterflies gathered at Natural Bridges State Park in Santa Cruz to overwinter in the eucalyptus groves. (One cannot see this now as monarchs in the West have declined 99 percent, according to the Center for Biological Diversity.) I was catalyzed by the sight of the monarchs bunched up like huge bags of laundry in the trees and by learning for the first time about their migration behavior—those in the West migrating to the remnant coastal forests, those in the East migrating to the mountains of central Mexico.

Surely such complex behavior could not be chalked up simply to instinct. It could only be, I thought, a manifestation of intelligence. And that launched me on a project that included visits with leading lepidopterists to the monarch refuges in Michoacán, Mexico, reading the most recent scientific papers on monarchs and studying the evolution of intelligence in nature across a broad span of species. This was a big question, and other questions clustered around it like magnetic bits in an Etch A Sketch. It wanted to be a poetic sequence—the long-form poem that helps resolve anxiety about challenges that plague shorter poems, like when does this poem start and when does it end? A poetic sequence just keeps going. I also liked the associations with the word "sequence," as it speaks to both the genetic code and the lifecycle of a star. So, the subject announced its form and on it went for sixty linked poems.

I've given you an origin story here about my artistic practice in bringing together science and poetry. In recent years I've been engaged in another practice that I will call applied poetics. Notable in this effort are two projects sponsored by Poets House, in which I worked with professionals at zoos, libraries, and science museums to create poetry programs that enhance science literacy and conservation values. The first involved curating a poetry installation at the Jacksonville [Florida] Zoo and Gardens, and the second, developing a poetry installation for the Milwaukee Public Library and Milwaukee Public Museum. Poet Katharine Coles has been an esteemed colleague in this work—and is certainly one of the smartest poets today working this field.

In the 1990s and 2000s the science documenting climate change and its consequences has become a central concern for anyone who cares about the future of life on Earth. "It's all about global warming, baby," writes C. D. Wright in her last book, *Casting Deep Shade* (2019). "We are the asteroid." At the same time, science denialism in America has risen to a terrifying crescendo. So, for me, interests that once seemed on the margin of cultural imperatives have now taken center stage and inform everything I write, whether prose or poetry.

I'll close with a new poem of mine that was first published in the January 2021 issue of *Scientific American* as part of a monthly feature curated by science writer Dava Sobel.

Letter to 2050

The Squamscott River
    grew lazy in early summer—
muskrat rose and dove
    heron swept the air and landed
and hemlocks that had survived
    another century's practice
of harvesting their bark
    were thriving. Some suffered
beaver girdles and the predation
    by woolly adelgids but still
the pileated woodpeckers
    found what they required
in the snags. This is how it was
    for us—pulling threads of hope
out of the air as if we had
    the skill to weave them
back into webs. We surprised
    ourselves when it worked—

so much needed to be undone.
　　And I promise you that
as paltry as our efforts
　　may seem to you—no.
I won't justify our failures.
　　The story of the alewives'
return—that's what I wanted
　　you to know because it helps
to think of desires that last
　　for centuries without being
satisfied. How far inland
　　did the alewives come,
I wondered, the dam removed
　　after three hundred years
and in the first year then
　　they came in a rush.
Locals could hear the gulls
　　gathered in the estuary
in their joy and the alewives
　　swam and swam to the reaches
of their ancestors—eleven miles
　　and three hundred years
of appetite for place
　　their genes remembered
and knew how to find.
　　The Abenaki offered
a welcome back ceremony.
　　And fishers gathered—human
cat and bird to feast
　　and the memory that had been
thwarted for centuries
　　became a fertile flow.

Science

Then it was the future, though what's arrived
isn't what we had in mind, all chrome and
cybernetics, when we set up exhibits
in the cafeteria for the judges
to review what we'd made of our hypotheses.

The class skeptic (he later refused to sign
anyone's yearbook, calling it a sentimental
degradation of language) chloroformed mice,
weighing the bodies before and after
to catch the weight of the soul,

wanting to prove the invisible
real as a bagful of nails. A girl
who knew it all made cookies from euglena,
a one-celled compromise between animal and plant,
she had cultured in a flask.

We're smart enough, she concluded,
to survive our mistakes, showing photos of farmland,
poisoned, gouged, eroded. No one believed
he really had built it when a kid no one knew
showed up with an atom smasher, confirming that

the tiniest particles could be changed
into something even harder to break.
And one whose mother had cancer (hard to admit now,
it was me) distilled the tar of cigarettes
to paint it on the backs of shaven mice.

She wanted to know what it took
a little vial of sure malignancy,
to prove a daily intake smaller
than a single aspirin could finish
something as large as a life. I thought of this

because, today, the dusky seaside sparrow
became extinct. It may never be as famous
as the pterodactyl or the dodo,
but the last one died today, a resident
of Walt Disney World where now its tissue samples

lie frozen, in case someday we learn to clone
one from a few cells. Like those instant dinosaurs
that come in a gelatin capsule—just add water
and they inflate. One other thing this
brings to mind. The euglena girl won first prize

both for science and, I think, for hope.

From *The Monarchs: A Poem Sequence*

1.
They hang in Santa Cruz by the hundreds of thousands
shingled over each other like dead leaves
high in the eucalyptus grove,
unable to move below fifty degrees,
but getting here from everywhere west of the Rockies
in time to winter out the cold.

Their navigation takes science—an animated
scrap of paper flying two thousand miles
for the first time each year (a nine-month
life) and making it. And art to know
to move when the idea strikes. Idea?
A butterfly idea? What could be smaller
or more frantic—yet correct. The beauties survive.

I like to think the same intelligence,
whatever makes the monarchs fly,
is at work in my friends who shed
jobs and marriages the way a eucalyptus
ruptures out of its bark as it grows.

Sometimes when I'm driving I forget the car—
riding thoughts instead into
what I should have said when he said,
"I guess you just don't want
to be married to anyone." Then I look up,
there's the sluice of the highway,
and I don't know how I got through the last city.

It's called unaware memory, what activates
when the body just does what it should.
No one remembers to accelerate,
which muscles to flex. The body
just does it because
the event is sufficiently rehearsed in the nerves.

18.
In Mexico where the eastern monarchs
gather for their winter sleep
a tide of fluttering orange and black
sweeping over the border and into the trees
of the central mountains, there is
such hunger that the campesinos,
though their fathers and mothers
believe the butterflies are
spirits of the dead returning,
must cut the forest for fuel and cropland.
Brush smoking, burned pits of stumps,
scrawny pony, burro tethered in the cut corn.
So much of the sanctuary has been lost
that experts have begun to issue
the usual decrees—how many years to go
before centuries of habit genetically
sealed in butterfly cells will be gone.
In the lofty remains of the cloud forest,
vigilantes guide the pilgrims under the dark canopy
of ancient trees and into the wind of butterfly wings.
In the heat of the afternoon
monarchs come down from their sleep
to huddle on the edges of streams and
meadow pools, trembling to stay warm,
and they sip, then sit, they fly off
until the air is a blizzard of orange.
The pilgrims watch quietly, lines of
schoolchildren from Mexico City,
scientists from Texas and California,
old women in rebozos leaning on the arms
of adult sons, tourists lugging
cameras and binoculars. And together
the visitors drink in the spectacle
with the great thirst they have brought
from their cities and towns, and it is

a kind of prayer, this meeting of our kind,
so uncertain about how to be
the creature we are, and theirs,
so clear in their direction.

Ann Fisher-Wirth

SCIENCE AND POETRY:
BEYOND THE RADISH SEEDS

By the road to the contagious hospital
under the surge of the blue
mottled clouds driven from the
northeast—a cold wind. Beyond, the
waste of broad, muddy fields
brown with dried weeds, standing and fallen

patches of standing water
the scattering of tall trees

All along the road the reddish
purplish, forked, upstanding, twiggy
stuff of bushes and small trees
with dead, brown leaves under them
leafless vines—

Lifeless in appearance, sluggish
dazed spring approaches—

They enter the new world naked,
cold, uncertain of all
save that they enter. All about them
the cold, familiar wind—

Now the grass, tomorrow
the stiff curl of wildcarrot leaf
One by one objects are defined—
It quickens: clarity, outline of leaf

But now the stark dignity of
entrance—Still, the profound change
has come upon them: rooted they
grip down and begin to awaken

THIS POEM, commonly known as "Spring and All," first occurs in
William Carlos Williams's *Spring and All*, a mélange of prose and
poetry published in 1923 by Robert McAlmon's Contact Publishing.
It is a wonderful example of the wedding of science with poetry—the
doctor passing by muddy fields on his way to a hospital for contagious
diseases, appreciating the seediness of spring, and aware, as he writes
in *Kora in Hell*, that "pathology . . . is a flower garden. . . . The study
of medicine is an inverted sort of horticulture" (77). "Spring and
All" is the first poem in *Spring and All* and breaks out of several pages
of prose celebrating "the imagination," which Williams describes as
the "single force" able "to refine, to clarify, to intensify that eternal
moment in which we alone live..." He fantasizes destroying the
"meager times," the "prohibitions," indeed "houses," "cities," "the
human race," so that "order and peace" may abound and the world
may be refreshed. And out of this rises the poem; out of this rises
the springtime. "Suddenly it is at an end. THE WORLD IS NEW."
    I did not study science when I was young. That's an understatement.
At Pomona College, when forced to sign up for botany and conduct
an experiment, I never got around to planting my radish seeds in
order to find out whether they grew better to silence, Bach, or the
Beatles; instead, I carried the seeds around in my pocket all semester.
Later, when my children were small, I learned to garden, because
that was something I could do while they napped, and then we could
walk to the garden center and stroll the aisles choosing flowers.
Then, some forty years ago, my life took me to living on a farm and
spending a lot of time in the woods—and eventually, after that, I
moved to Mississippi, where I created the University of Mississippi's
interdisciplinary minor in environmental studies. This year, I am
principal investigator on a National Endowment for the Humanities
planning grant, "Environmental Literacy and Engagement in North
Mississippi," which involves close collaboration among humanities,

social sciences, and natural sciences to redesign the year-long introductory course sequence and develop a lot of outreach and internship opportunities for our students. Working with my colleagues in different departments, especially biology, has taught me a great deal. So has teaching the mandatory gateway course "Humanities and the Environment," and several other environmental literature courses, in which we study writers including Rachel Carson, Elizabeth Kolbert, David George Haskell, J. Drew Lanham, Janisse Ray, and the other *Poetry and Science* contributors. As coeditor, with Laura-Gray Street, of *The Ecopoetry Anthology* (2013)—which is 625 pages of American nature poetry and ecopoetry from Whitman to the present—I have become aware of the tremendous range and diversity among writers for whom the other-than-human world is of pre-eminent importance, and who write about it with a scientific accuracy that reveals the natural world's specificity, variety, and abundance. In "Jubilate Agno," the eighteenth-century British poet Christopher Smart writes, "God make gardeners better nomenclators"—a line that I take to refer to the quest for art and precision in naming the ten thousand things of this world.

I've always loved the metaphor of Indra's net—the vast, jeweled net into which all things are woven—and the realization that any slightest movement on the net ripples throughout creation. It is wonderful that recent work like Merlin Sheldrake's book *Entangled Life: How Fungi Make Our Worlds, Change Our Minds, and Shape Our Futures* (2020) shows how this interconnectivity and interdependency extend throughout the entire living world. Once more, science is discovering what poetry and religion have long known: in some deep and real sense, we are one.

❦

I have lived in Mississippi for thirty-two years. The state suffers from severe environmental degradation that cannot be separated from its history of poverty and racial oppression; there is nothing pristine about it. Yet it also possesses great natural beauty.

Here are two poems about Mississippi:

Winter Day on the Whirlpool Trails

Where the power lines go through,
the red clay gullies and pits, not even
privet can grow fast enough to bind it.
We clamber down and up, and down and up,
and turn to enter the woods. Further along,
we come to broken glass, old brown bottles
nearly buried, a toilet choked with brush,
bricks, some pipes, some turquoise plastic coiling.
It's just like that, here—people dump things
and they sink, protrude rusty and jagged
from the mud, or block the trail,
stained with leaf mold. To the side,
some withered Southern red oaks,
a blackjack oak, knobby trunks of trees
choked by spiraling vines—Virginia creeper,
poison ivy—and leafless sweetgums
with their little sci-fi seedpods.
Everywhere rotting, everywhere teeming,
moss like emeralds on the stumps,
the hollow logs. This is my home, this leaf-duff
and dereliction, where look—a vulture wheels
above the cedars, searching for what stinks.
Where a first tender violet, blooming
by my feet before Valentine's Day,
signifies the seasons are in heat.
The great blue heron's not here today,
standing motionless among the reeds.
But a turtle slides off a distant log, and sunlight
scatters like shot across the scum-slicked pond.

Credo

But the cardinal, the birdsong, do not need you,
to pulse forward into the light. The peaches do not need you,
to swell and soften, dark with the sugars of summer.
Oh you can be the flesh their juices run down,
but you do not make the seed nor the earth it grows in.

And the artist, what is she? The one whose hands are empty.
Who says—though to what, I do not know—
speak through me as you will.
Who calls the made thing out of the sheltering darkness.

                              Now the day is full of leaves.
After the rain, the sky is low and white as ash.
The ragged garden spikes and trembles.

ADDITIONAL POEMS BY ANN FISHER-WIRTH

Catalpa

This tree is older than Columbus. Ten years ago my honors students standing in a ring could barely get their arms around it. I took their picture—hands joined, cheeks against the rough wood. Mostly they loved it but one guy told my friend who supervised his lab, *She made us hug a tree. It was the worst class ever.*

When I think of the tree as a sapling, my mind enters a great quiet. Before the Depression, the yellow fever, before the burning of Oxford, before the University Greys left their classrooms for the battlefield and died or were wounded to a man at Pickett's Charge, and before Princess Hoka of the Chickasaws set out with her people on the Trail of Tears, this tree sank its roots deep and deeper into the nurturing ground. Generations moved about beneath its boughs, spoke and loved and died as it grew.

And here it is, still, in the clattering present.

Ten years ago I could walk around it, smell it, stroke the lichens on its bark. If I put my hand into the hollow in its trunk right near the ground, it was always cold, always comforting, no matter how brutal the summer, as if some dark, mysterious lungs kept serenely breathing.

Now fences surround it, stakes hold up its branches. No longer do art majors loll on the benches and smoke at the little table under its big-leaf shade. A sign warns NO CLIMBING: KEEP OFF. Still, every spring, wet tender leaves unfurl on branches jagged as broken bones, and the tree bursts out in a froth of white petals.

And every spring, the preachers line the sidewalk near the tree, and thrust their Bibles as we pass by. *Repent and be saved,* they say. *Turn or burn.* I want to tell them, *Turn around, turn around, and look at the tree.*

Val Corsaglia, Italian Piemonte

We walked away from the village of Corsaglia along a trail that led through lush,

Species loss

nearly impenetrable oak, hazelnut, and chestnut woods, past ancient stone houses

ocean acidification

and shepherds' huts, beside a rushing stream. When we began to walk it was softly

ocean "dead zones"

raining. The rain soon stopped, but the mist and cool soft air remained. Everywhere

global freshwater crisis

wildflowers—buttercups, daisies, scabiosa with its purple tufts, Johnny jump-ups,

deforestation

button ferns, wild geraniums, wild strawberries. Once, when the river

consequent soil erosion

curved away, a meadow opened up to our left, and it was so richly flowering

colony collapse disorder

that I could only think of the millefleurs foregrounds of medieval paintings,

fertilizers and herbicides, chemically toxic soil

the thousand small flowers springing up around the Christ child

Elizabeth Bradfield

GRAPPLING WITH THE INEFFABLE; SCIENCING THE SCIENCE; BLURRING LINES

THERE ARE MANY THINGS that poetry and science have in common: a search to understand how the world works; detailed and precisely documented observation; an openness to surprise, abstraction (whether artistic/informational/graphic/metaphoric), and the ephemeral (now! no, now!) as a way of visualizing a question; acceptance of complexity; dedication to providing a path for others to retrace the process of comprehension.

And more. And more. In some ways, I am frustrated by the question that underpins this conversation—science and poetry have never been that far apart. Only recently have we divided STEM from STEAM. But, as with all, the question, really, is about how. *How, when, in what way…* These are very individual questions that might lead us into new relationships and ways of knowing in our answers.

For some poets, writing about science is a way of grappling with the ineffable—of bridging mind, memory, and soul. It's about the way instruments can validate processes beyond what we can comprehend with our five senses: strange attractions at an atomic scale, reactions within beakers and vials, the interactions triggered by pheromones.

The formal possibilities of the scientific method, too, have their pull: hypothesis, experimentation/observation, conclusion (and, buried within that, my favorite part of any scientific paper: suggestions for further research). The attraction here is both formal and conceptual: formally, the scientific method suggests shape; conceptually, it is a tidy system waiting to be exploded through other ways of knowing.

In my lived experience, science has always been part of and also, interestingly, at odds with natural history. Science provides a way to observe and understand the nuances of birds, lichens, whales, and all to which I seek to be attuned. The information science has given me has deepened what I see and hear when I look and listen. Yet natural history doesn't answer everything, and it also doesn't always seem as "sciencey" as other fields; it's just attention and observation, less about designed experiments and more about understanding what's influencing a falcon, seal, or shadbush in the moment. I seek to be attuned. Attending is all. Through math, statistics, wind, scent, memory, story, and more.

I want, here, to reach into two different ways that science pervades my own personal poetic practice: first, there is a "sciencing of science" and, second, a dedication to thinking ecologically and socially about interconnection and the importance of "clear looking."

❧

What often puzzles me about the poetry/science conversations I find myself drawn to and fumbling within is the broadness of "science." I assume, here, that I'm in the company of poets. As such, we understand the language and the labels of our field (confessionalism, objectivism, formalism, etc.) as well as how poetic definitions and categories are helpful in addition to being problematic. But I'm not sure we, as poets, engage with the same nuance when it comes to "science."

For all the debates about what poetry *is*, I think we also need to define what "science" is in these conversations—not overall, but for each poet, each poem. In each instance.

Science is vast and contains many approaches and philosophies (multitudes?). Are we talking formulas and math? Chemical interactions? The ability to recognize the smell of a particular species of zooplankton in a slick on the water? Aptitude with a scalpel? A knack for reading body language? Stats to predict market futures?

From mathematics to chemistry to field biology to medicine to sociology to economics: science. That's like trying to lump all poetry together, when we know there's spoken word, ecopoetics, docu-poetics, L=A=N=G=U=A=G=E poetry, formalism, confessionalism

…and hybrids and warpings and permutations of them all.

As a poet who "does science" with animals in the field, I will confess that I often feel less "sciencey" than my colleagues skilled in PCR assays, climate modeling, or radiology. My science still involves working old technologies (binoculars, hand lenses, paper and pencil) and techniques (observation and careful note-taking) while watching and wondering. It's a science still widely available to all with time, a few basic tools, curiosity and desire. However, what direct observation has taught us—as scientists, poets, and life-students of animals and plants—is incalculable.

The point is that the conventions and conversations of science vary from field to field. The questions, opportunities, peoples, histories, and problems, too. Fumblings and discoveries and the lives of the scientists themselves are both beautiful and inspiring as well as deeply problematic and embedded in the prejudices of the societies that spawned them. Let me repeat it: science is not pure, not "apart."

And here's where my poet-mind perks up: Part of my poetic practice, I have recently come to realize, is to unofficially work as an anthropologist of field biology. To "science the science"—put an analytical lens onto researchers, field work, and theories. To try to see the lenses *through which we see.*

Sexism, racism, ageism, misogyny, homophobia, ableism, and other bigotries are part of the history (and present) of science—not necessarily through its methodologies, but absolutely through its practitioners (them/us), which includes the ways studies develop between colleagues, the questions researchers are willing to entertain (and fund), the conclusions reached from the evidence at hand, the mentorships offered, the fellowships encouraged, the "Hey, come stay with me rent free" offers that are offered. I still know scientists who are puzzled by the drive to diversify science, who think the work is "pure." But the work is never purified of its workers.

As we all know, science can be harmful as well as helpful. The syphilis experiments at the Tuskegee Institute are a glaring example, but there are so many more, and more subtle, instances out there. If access to traditional hunting of seals is prevented due to "population management," what does that mean for Indigenous communities?

If Black hands are not recognized by "automatic" faucets, who gets to be clean in airport bathrooms? If a team of botanists drops into Madagascar from Norway without taking the time to work with local organizations to understand dynamics on the ground ("helicopter biology") or to invite local people to participate, what are the long-term consequences to conservation and communication?

"It'll be fine" has never been a good response to "What is the cost?" And we've failed again and again to calculate the cost of our research and the policies (or absences) research has led to. I don't want to claim, here, an authority or depth of knowledge that is capable of listing all the wrongs of science. That's not my study. But I can see and state where these larger questions have come into direct confrontation with local issues in my own experience as a poet and field researcher.

For example: How do we weigh the rights and needs of North Atlantic Right Whales and Lobster fisherfolk?* North Atlantic Right Whales are dying because of us, both because of our historical fisheries and our present presence in the water. No one wants to see these animals disappear. No one. But the dynamic is not simple. How do we weigh the needs of animals and the needs of people (another animal)? How do the human-needs and animal-needs get supported or seen by the people not directly involved as fishers on the water or as scientists grappling with entanglement?

Honestly, I don't know.

Science quickly slides into management, and that's…hard. It's full of unions and lobbies and historic arguments and decisions I am terrified to wade into. Terrified. Because I have dear friends who fish, dear friends who disentangle whales from fishing gear.

And, really, we all know each other (biologists, fishers), but the national news wants us to be in opposition. Social media wants to lob science and emotion, both, as bombs into either camp. But how can we—the scientists, the fishers—live that way? We live in the same

---

* A note on capitalization: While it's not conventional to capitalize the names of species, in this essay, when the mention seemed particular enough to be intimate and singular, I have done so. This is an attempt to recognize the animals' individuality and beingness. I have not done so in quoted texts or in cases when the mention seemed more general. It's an imperfect gesture but one that hopes to move toward honoring the nonhuman.

communities. We prep our boats for the same storms. We assess the same sea conditions, albeit with different aims in mind. We see the same warming sea temperatures and fear their consequences, track them obsessively. We both want work and "goodness"—and by these I mean a semi-religious idea of work and contribution and morality—to be in alignment.

So often, we are at odds with one another. What do we do?

Two days ago, I drove (yes, in my hybrid car) to a spot on Cape Cod where I knew at this time of year I might see whales. I sat in the cold lot for a while and then: *THERE!* I texted a young naturalist who was living in town for her first winter and had never seen Right Whales, and I also texted a "sea hag" (one of a group of matriarchs I am lucky to be satellite to). They drove in. All of us lifted binoculars and watched Right Whales at a far distance breathing, breaking the surface, sometimes slapping a huge paddle-shaped flipper onto the water, sometimes fluking for a deeper dive.

If this had been a movie, you'd have been bored. But it was thrilling. We knew that we were watching something rare. We had information, binoculars, imagination, time. Right Whales are one of the most endangered large whales on the planet, and we were watching nine of them scattered across our view. Still, it took story to sense the moment's awe. It took imagination to really "see" what we were seeing.

And this sight that thrilled us is a threat to others.

If another endangered calf loses a life because of a ship strike? If a breeding female becomes entangled in legally set fishing gear that, in the end, kills her? If my neighbor loses his livelihood? What then? I know I've strayed from our opening question and conversation. But I want all of you, if you don't already, to feel how difficult the reconciliations between "scientific knowing" and "neighborhood" are. To consider the consequences of science on a human, local scale, and to imagine how poetry might do that essential work.

Who gets to talk about the Vaquita in the northern Gulf of California (why is it called the Gulf of California?)? If we're talking about the Spotted Owl in old-growth forests of the Pacific Northwest, where is the acknowledgment of Indigenous caretaking of that forest? Acknowledgment of the loss of those caretakers through the legacy of colonialism? Science, how do you embrace Traditional Ecological Knowledge? (You're doing better, you're doing better.)

Science (and poetry) can be exclusionary as well as revelatory. Often, the best scientific breakthroughs come when a researcher not in the "majority" sees something differently: gender relations among primates, biases within facial recognition, connections between human and ecological health.

I'm interested in those stories. I think poetry can help keep science honest.

To that end, I want to share a poem from my book *Once Removed* (2015). The first half of the poem lists some historical and contemporary scientific theories that, to me, seem questionable. In the second half, I reference a video about a Lion named Christian that, in 2008, went viral on YouTube. I wanted, here, to look at the ways science got things "wrong" and also how I, an enlightened and thinking soul of the twenty-first century, as well as a kind of scientist, might also get things wrong:

Misapprehensions of Nature

That bees are improper
          because they have a queen
no king. That crows plant

acorns, twist them into soil,
          properly spaced, to serve
as future roosts and manta rays

wrap divers in the dark
          blankets (*mantilla*)
of their wings.

That dolphins
          love us, that deer love us,
and the kit brought in and given milk

is just as happy. That we can know
            what it is for a fox
to be happy.

                    ❧

Two men bought a lion
            at Harrods, reared it
in their small apartment,

released it (reluctantly) to savannah.
            And then, years later,
sure that it would know them,

went and called its pet name
            into the grasses.
It ran toward them.

That they would be mauled.
            That perhaps they should
be mauled. But it

tumbled them, licked their faces:
            Everyone was crying.
            We were crying,
even the lion was nearly crying.

This poem came from the fact that the action in the video went against everything my biologist-self expected and had trained herself to know: "We think animals love us, but they don't." It went against everything I taught people, when out in the field, about how humans and wild nonhumans see each other. It called into question my caution of assigning "human" emotions or acknowledging the possibility of equitable emotional connection between wild animals and humans. The video refuted it all. That Lion *loved* those guys; he remembered them. In essence, my science was challenged. I was made a fool (and gladly). Dramatizing that seemed interesting and important.

Recently a couple of moments have given me pause as a semi-scientist and a poet. I was listening to a researcher in the literary humanities talking about invisibility with an astrophysicist. (Both are men, and I respect and truly like them both, but their gender is worth noting given how historically male-centric science is.) The astrophysicist talked about properties of light and what allowed something to be seen; in his examples, he called metaphorically upon snakes, bears, trees, and other earthbound creatures to help us understand his highly theoretical field. The humanities professor talked about imagined worlds: the believable world of Jane Austen and the believable and yet acknowledged-as-fantastical world of Tolkien. These were different kinds of "seeing" and knowing to them both. A vital part of me was engaged with this talk, sparked to it. And yet, I was dissatisfied and cranky. Why? I think it's because the metaphors each was using didn't feel like they fully stretched toward my knowledge and understanding of the world. I asked about the sought invisibility of animals, such as the "cryptic clicking" of mammal-hunting Orca as they seek to disguise themselves from prey; I asked about the "passing" of people who wish to escape their sexuality, class, or race in order to move into different conversations or avoid prejudice. At the moment, I was aware of how hugely limited our discussion was by the generality of our engagement.

When we used the words "science," "invisibility," and "humanities," what did we mean? So much. So vastly much. Yet no one had detailed the particulars. Again, the problem lay in what "science" meant. The astrophysicist wasn't talking about biology, though he used images of snakes and bears to illustrate his examples of different ways of seeing. The humanist wasn't talking about biological processes or social pressures. They were happy in the science-world they'd defined without fully defining it, and it would have been painful and awkward to challenge their paradigm (and indeed when I fumbled toward doing so, I was met with silence). "Poetry and Science" as a topic is just too broad...and yet it is still so necessary a conversation to have. Any of the messiness of this essay, any of its fumblings, must be linked to the awkwardness of the premise itself.

I want, here, to pause and invite the voice of Alexis Pauline Gumbs, whose *Undrowned: Black Feminist Lessons from Marine Mammals* (2020) has challenged and goaded me to think more creatively about the conversations between natural history and human understanding. In *Undrowned*, Gumbs offers specific and accurate natural history descriptions of various marine mammals to illustrate her investigation into Black identity (particularly female identity). As one example, Gumbs looks at how Right Whale Dolphins hunt in the ocean's deep scattering layer, and she explores what that teaches us about how to "stay deep when distracting distractions distract us (like racists being racist for racist reasons)" (129).

Was I resistant to her use of marine mammals as metaphor? Yes, I was. Too often, I've seen whales, seals, and other marine creatures used as some easy proxy for…what? An alliance, a voyage of the self, a quick and potent reference that might move anyone. Alexis Pauline Gumbs challenged me. I pushed against her voice again and again, in *Undrowned*, as she asked us both to look at the actual lives of walruses, dolphins, beaked whales, and manatees, and to consider human lives. She does the research and work to fully "see" these beings in their own worlds and needs. With that informed awareness, she asks us to seriously consider ourselves and the flawed society that holds us. Alexis Pauline Gumbs. Not a scientist. A poet. Someone who dared me on all levels to think more widely/wildly about how the lives of animals could help people know the nuances of Black life. From Ferguson to the Middle Passage. Alexis Pauline Gumbs: thank you. Your lessons are ongoing and I continue to study.

❦

Since I wrote "Misapprehensions of Nature," there have been more and more scientists talking about the sentience and, well, *emotions* of nonhuman beings—trees sharing resources, whales in mourning, crows who have affinities and distastes for particular people. We're not heading back toward the pathetic fallacy…but maybe we are? Maybe the Romantics were more right than we've given them credit for. Maybe science is now coming around to poetry, with eyes open to the wide diversity of relationships and ways of being that are possible.

My science—the one I've practiced and been adjacent to for the past twenty-some years—is the science of animal biology (particularly marine mammals) and ecology. The lives of nonhuman beings—how they operate independently of the human world, and how our human world (built, social, or political) engages with them—is the topic of about 80 percent of my conversation most days at home. (Almost all of my local friends and community are biologists and naturalists, and I sometimes forget that this is not true for all people. Don't you all talk about bristle worms and bioaccumulation over lunch? When you're out walking together, isn't your primary conversation topic the recent and unusual number of Torpedo Rays on the beach or the question of how to best gather and preserve scat samples?) All of the biologists I know have deep feelings about the work they do—feelings that the conventions of science tell them to keep out of the published papers, the study design. My poems often stem from an overheard comment from my biologist friends, becoming a conversation that tugs me because it needs to be pulled into other relations, other queries. These poems often blur the edges of science/poetry itself.

The writings of Robin Wall Kimmerer and Richard Nelson shine for me as models in this work. Both scientists, in their writings they hold up the importance of story and data, clear thinking and emotional resonance. Both honor the connection between the human and the nonhuman. Head and heart. Here's Richard Nelson:

> Sometimes I wonder if I'll ever hear or see anything as it truly is, or if a lifetime is only enough to begin learning how to watch and listen. . . . Science is a wonderful tool for examining, measuring, and describing the world, but its explanations are sometimes no more convincing and far less wise than the ancient stories or the mystical imagination. Perhaps certain things about the world are best discovered by engaging the senses completely and leaving the analytical mind at rest. (*The Island Within*, 1989, p. 84)

In *Gathering Moss* (2003), Robin Wall Kimmerer embraces two ways of knowing that have been held apart: "An Onondaga elder once explained to me that plants come to us when they are needed. If we show them respect by using them and appreciating their gifts they will grow stronger. They will stay with us as long as they are respected. But if we forget about them, they will leave" (161). Plants show themselves? They come to us? Such thinking is counter to all I've been taught, but I believe it and I know that Kimmerer is right. I'm trying to learn a more expansive sense of science through her words.

Eva Saulitis is the final poet-scientist I'd like to point to as a model for how to build new bridges of understanding between science and other ways of knowing. Her book *Leaving Resurrection: Chronicles of a Whale Scientist* (2008) details her research as a Killer Whale biologist in the wake of the 1989 Exxon Valdez oil spill. In the book, Saulitis blends science, memoir, and—in one stunning moment—poetry in the tradition of the First Peoples of what is now named Prince William Sound on the maps. In describing the origins of whales, walking us through the ages and epochs of evolution, Saulitis uses the patterns and style of traditional Alaska Native literary forms, specifically Tlingit oral poetry—the repetitions and repeated place-markers of language that would be familiar to anyone who has spent time with Haida, Tlingit, Tsimshian, or Eyak literature. And, importantly, Saulitis says up front how and why this mode of telling is important: it's important because these whales are part of the culture of the First Peoples of the area, and vice versa. The relationship dictated the form. It is science, yes, but also human relation, each teaching the other through their ways of telling. This complicated dance is something we can learn from as poets *and* as scientists. From pages 182 to 185:

> I push the buttons of other killer whale researcher friends, not because I'm interested in Native knowledge and mythology of killer whales—we're all interested—but because they think I privilege it. . . . Alaska Native people have been living on this coast for thousands of years, since, as they say, "time immemorial."

Compared to the rest of us, their ties to this place are old. Killer whales have been swimming in the ocean in relatively the same forms for the last five million years. Compared to humans, whales and their ties to the sea are ancient. . . .

I'll practice by telling a story. Craig narrated the bones of it to me one day last week. It's the scientific creation story of the killer whale. Let me tell it as elder Willie Marks told the Tlingit killer whale origin story in the anthology *Haa Shuká, Our Ancestors*. It's poetry, his telling, with its pauses and repetitions. And it's a transformation story. Paleontologists believe that the evolution of whales represents the most complete transformation undergone by any mammal.

> Once, in the distant time,
> 53 million years ago,
> the ancestors of killer whales lived on land.
> They lived on land,
> those hippo-ancestors of killer whale.
> Over millions of years, they gradually lost
> those hippo-like limbs.
> This happened in the ancient Tethys Sea,
> where Pakistan is now. Some of this land
> is now at the top of the Himalayas.
> That's where you'll find
> those sediments today.
> Anthracotheres, they were called,
> the proto-killer whales, medium sized,
> piggish beasts
> with four-hooved toes
> on each front foot.

Listening to Saulitis's poem, there's the thrum of evolution and also the thrum of storytelling—not just storytelling but the telling of land, sea, and peoples (human and nonhuman) who live wholly in a place. And, of course, we need both. We need deeply envisioned storytelling that embodies science and self and how all our ways of knowing might flow into and become a greater acknowledgment. We need TEK (Traditional Ecological Knowledge) to shape science, anthropology to influence biology, and more. We need the web to be complicated, interlinked, and messy.

In my own work, I want to use poems as a way to explore the emotional world behind science, to give worry and wonder a voice. To blend experience, knowledge, and story. Sometimes I try to do that through wryness and information. There are many poems in which I confront what we know head-on. But there's another way of knowing, one that drifts and queries and acknowledges all the contradictory skeins of knowing. This, I think, ultimately, like Saulitis's work, is the poem that is speaking most importantly into a new or oppositional space—one that is aware of the pathetic fallacy, of the beauty of data, yet seeks another way of holding emotionality and fact within the living body.

This next poem moves from scientific awareness of hydrography, geology, atmospheric pollution, bioaccumulation, and what it means on a very personal level:

Permeable
  —after Leah Wong

> Below us: water (fresh lens). And
> below that: a different water
> (salt soused). This youngest end
> of a glacier-spat spit,
>   this outwash plain,
> grains permeable, percolating,
>
>   angular, rough, tilted
> piled & drifted into
>   dunes, swales. Space
> between the planes. Slip and seep.

How does it hold? How are
         we held? As we bustle, as we duck
                  whatever current licks
         at us. A comfort to river

                  my own salt through a pond
         which is an open eye of the water
body (aquifer) a well sucks
         from under backyard sand
                  (pull too deep & you'll
         draw salt). We float, placid,

      though not untouched by what falls,
         heavy, from seeming-clear sky into
                  nymph-body, fish-body. Or what
         fins up from salt-depth, toothed. Or
riptides (diver lost this summer
         & the body held two days
                  before washed ashore). Sorrow,

         I have felt you, seeping
                  as the pond's larger body seeps,
         flows slow, finally rivers out
a few feet below mean high into larger
         water—you've seen those small rivers,
underworld-cool, vein-like and branching
         into our porous, dangerous world.

In "Permeable," I'm less interested in what science can teach poetry
than in what poetry can teach science. I'm interested in how the
two fields can intermingle, how complexity can be invited not as
confusion but as, let's say, a clear wrangling. I want it laid out so
its various elements, their dovetailings and divergences, can be
considered consciously, not just bumbled through or glossed over for
a surface clarity.

In the end, what I think is important is the capacity of poetry to honor the power of unknowing, of wonder based in and drawn from a life of deep study and observation. What is certainty? What is the value of certainty? I'm less and less certain.

❧

I'll end with two other poems from *Once Removed* that dance with knowledge and unknowing. I hope we all leave this conversation ready to complicate our ways of knowing, ready to embody them.

We All Want to See a Mammal

We all want to see a mammal.
Squirrels & snowshoe hares don't count.
Voles don't count. Something, preferably,
that could do us harm. There's a long list:
bear, moose, wolf, wolverine. Even porcupine
would do. The quills. The yellowed
teeth & long claws.
                          Beautiful here: Peaks, avens,
meltwater running its braided course. But we want
to see a mammal. Our day our lives incomplete
without a mammal. The gaze of something
unafraid, that we're afraid of, meeting ours
before it runs off.
                          Linneaus was called
indecent when he named them. Plenty
of other commonalities (hair, live young,
a proclivity to plot). But no. Mammal.
Maman. Breasted & nippled
& warm, warm, warm.

Right Whale: Death as Spectacle

The bulk ashore not yet fetid, but surely
close. Tire tracks deep in sand where tractors
tried to haul it up, chain around the tail stock.

There was a steady stream of visitors, for who
wouldn't want to see or didn't feel obliged
to stand near and take measure of

a right whale on the beach? Still, I don't know
that it was anything good in me, anything kind
or gentle that made me think my grandmother,

visiting, would want to be there. We trudged
into a hard wind toward the yellow flags
staked around books of flensed blubber.

Biologists clambered the ribs and bonnet,
measuring, cutting in, digging for cause.
I was young. Bulk and death fascinated me, but

my grandmother had already put behind her tonnages
of grief. The colors of the flesh—black skin, white fat,
red meat—were steeped in late fall light. Baleen listed

from its jaw, nodding to wind, waves, footsteps over the body.
How beautiful, I thought. How lucky. How sad.
This was spectacle and, too, a reprobation of spectacle.

Her face was composed in the soft blank of looking.
Really, I have no idea what she thought.

Allison Adelle Hedge Coke

POETRY/SCIENCE: LAB COATS FOR HOUSE COATS

I'LL START OUT WITH THIS STATEMENT: Science is a natural way of perceiving and witnessing for the purpose of knowing. It's trial and error, experiment, and it's given us all sorts of healing and culinary wonders, some from otherwise deadly sources. It's brought us to understand our ways of being, to match our ways of knowing from stories that predate our existence by a stream of generations before us and our surrounding environments' and ecosystems' dictations and needs in reciprocity. We are symbiotic, or not. When not, we are oftentimes completely out of balance, out of kinship. Contemporary science attempts to reason with what older cultures around the world have already proven and known and have the scientific knowledge built within cultural practices and understandings—within doings. This knowing, as well, is essential to our survival on the planet, our beingness. Poets and scientists share a main line—curiosity. It inspires and activates us wholly.

I came into the world in a familial knowing of science being a part of everything. Be it a cultural science or contemporary knowledge of science.

If you asked my father a question, he might answer you over years, each incident bringing in some sense of older knowing and some sense of perception or perceiving. Math and science were integral parts of our traditional familial knowledge in our home. Raised by a storyteller and singer who was born in 1922, whose parents were born in 1878 and 1882 (the latter, his mother, a root doctor and midwife), by my father, a storyteller who married a musician who worked with him on the polio epidemic as some of the first physical therapists in the world. They continued their work in hospital until my father used his cobbled-together World War II G.I. Bill B.A. in chemistry (because he was spending time playwriting) to return to work as an analytical chemist, as he had been as a layman, at Phillips, before he met my mother. His first hire outside of field labor, or riding fence, and military service.

We wore lab coats in our home as house coats. Everything had to do with cultural kinship, and everything was, truly, related.

We interwove a traditional sense of science and modern science due to my father's work. We could have survived alone in the elements for some time—any of us as kids—with the knowledge of survival and nature hacks we were immersed in. And on the other hand, the periodic table was not an uncommon chart in our home and seemed to us common knowledge. Science, physics, astronomy, medical terminology, physiology, chemistry were as typical a conversation as original stories or songs.

Actually, they were an element of inclusion in all of this and in the way my father spoke of any other feature of childhood, steeped in oratory and cultured by an older generation. Science has always been, it just wasn't a separate study or discipline thought to be modern until more recent times.

Early on, in our home, my father taught me square roots and basic algebraic equations while he was studying refresher courses for a job. He kept telling me to do the puzzles to keep from bothering him too much. He would write problems on paper and explain what to do and have me solve them, preschool-aged. We used numbers to play binary code puzzles and other games, and we were well aware that when leaves fell, they were filled with anthocyanin.

We also knew the traditional stories of the same trees.

We knew mound cities were laid out in accordance with stellar events and cycles in the heavens. We understood physics and astronomy as a way to speak about everyday occurrences like friction or meteor showers we camped underneath. And the stories that went along with those occurrences as well. The flow of water, of air, the thermals birds soar, migrate, and sail as murmurations, when we went to bird councils, hawk councils with my father.

Just as poetry is life, science is. It depends what science you're relating to. What is from a deeper cultural knowing that's existed for tens of thousands of generations, or from contemporary learning and accumulation of explanations and knowing, from perceiving from outside one's own culture. Like story and culture, they're inextricable.

Another typical instance of reflection for us is time-skipping, in the family, or portal opening, of knowing or perceiving. This is how portent, or premonition, was explained to us, as a ripple occurring, so that if somebody is doing something that's significant in this day and time, the generations that walk with us in our DNA, in our genetic code, feel that in the past and have premonitions of what's happening today. And so, we're relating to the future generations before us.

This was taught to us as children.

Just yesterday, monarch-seekers went where they normally might be immersed within nearly 50,000 monarchs in this season and only saw one or two. My works all deal with change, the planet, its peoples in different forms, and the effect that man has had on the devastation of our planet and its many original cultures and beings. My forthcoming book, *Look at This Blue* (2022), is a one-hundred-page poem immersed in my love for the natural world and the catastrophic loss we are existing within. It's an indictment and a love poem for my home base, California.

It's what we do as poets. We translate the world through our curiosity and through things learned. Much like the life of a scientist.

My first poetry professor was Arthur Sze, and he came from science as well. His parents fully expected him to stay in the sciences they worked in, and at work studying at MIT. And from his time as a student there, he began also studying poetry with Josephine Miles and Denise Levertov and abandoned MIT for UC Berkeley to study poetry.

I related to him in his work immediately. (This is when I was an undergrad at the Institute of American Indian Arts many years ago.) I want to share a poem of his that demonstrates, much as I was saying, that poetry is a part of life. It's how we live and translate the world and sciences, unimmersed or immersed within all of this.

This is "Net Light" by Arthur Sze, and I wish you could hear him read this. He gives just stunning readings. If you don't know his work, please look him up and listen to some of his readings.

Net Light

Poised on a bridge, streetlights
on either shore, a man puts
a saxophone to his lips, coins
in an upturned cap, and a carousel

in a piazza begins to turn:
where are the gates to paradise?
A woman leans over an outstretched
paper cup—leather workers sew

under lamps: a belt, wallet, purse—
leather dyed maroon, beige, black—
workers from Seoul, Lagos, Singapore—
a fresco on a church wall depicts

the death of a saint: a friar raises
both hands in the air—on an airplane,
a clot forms in a woman's leg
and starts to travel toward her heart—

a string of notes riffles the water;
and, as the clot lodges, at a market
near lapping waves, men unload
sardines in a burst of argentine light.

So throughout the poem, we have this kinship value and the physics and physiology of people on the planet. And what's happening within the body and its effect on everything around it, including the notes in the air and the clot in the leg. Quite beautiful work that he does consistently.

And while I was in graduate school, I had the great advantage of having Alison Hawthorne Deming come in as a visiting poet. She had won the Whitman prize. We were quite impressed with her work then and I remain so today. She had spent some time with eagles and, like us, being raised going to bird councils. I was all over it.

Here is a poem of Alison's from *The Monarchs*:

22.
Redwoods. At night they take
the headlights without blinking,
their thousand-year-old patience
disturbed only slightly by lightning
or wildfire. To them the sorrow
of the celibate fathers is the same

as the sorrow of the missionized tribes.
They are satisfied to drink what rain
can be wrung from the billowing fog.
They tolerate nattering creatures
inhabiting their bark and branches.
Their hearts rise straight through their bodies

and are not harmed by hardening.
Unable to hear, see, smell, or taste,
they know when to drop their lower branches,
broaden their root anchor, when to
climb and bud. The redwoods, without
liquid hydrogen or God, have mastered time,

with their tracheids and sieve tubes,
their angel cells catch and release the light.

And I'll end with a closing poem from one of my books. They're
all climate change to a degree. They all deal with physics to a degree.
They all deal with the built world and the natural world. And one
book, *Off-Season City Pipe*, is a labor collection that begins and ends
with eclipses. This is "Waiting for the Last Lunar Eclipse, 2004":

I dreamed of a sudden eclipse
revealing unexpected stars
causing me to shift in my sleep,

remember mounds assembled,

basketful by basketful—the building.
Various earths carefully compiled
commemorating dead immortal

underneath compelling skies.

A woman peeling slivers
from a great ball
hanging loose leavings
like locust leaf-silver.

Then stars filled sky—radiant.

While earth wrapped moon in rose
I imagined night briefly breaking
light barriers like pulses, in other

daytimes, somewhere far beyond.

Here in the muck of morning,
where gray slates sky
and drizzle threatens,
Oneonta, New York.

A star, or two, may hover blind.

Constantly preparing plenty
wholly pondering day,
hoping to light the world like us,
and we in welcome wait.

Additional Poems by Allison Adelle Hedge Coke
from *Look at This Blue*

Blue Whale

Blue Whale   *alongside Monterey, San Diego, Baja*
    gentle giant heaviest animal to ever live on earth, twice Argentinosaurus
        ship strikes kill eleven per year, US West coast, with ship increase
population will be depleted, noise, military testing, sonic battery,
      chemicals, plastics — blue with belly full of plastics —
        krill, anchovie, tiny fish, tiny crustaceans absorb micro-plastics
            a blue whale eats between 2 and 4 tons of krill per day

bluecurls

Hidden Lake bluecurls   *from Hidden Lake, San Jacintos, Riverside County*

                                   on the shores of a single vernal pool, ephemeral
            trampling by hikers, sight seekers, endangers
                each flower a hairy calyx with pointed sepals
                                        tubular corona
                                        fifty flowers might fit on a penny
                                        a member of the mint family
                            delisting 2018, seeds stored in seed bank
            vulnerable

Chance Mutation

Mutant blue-eyed coyotes   chance mutation

       baby blues in nine coyotes suggesting proliferation
              silvery brown-backed with icy blue eyes
      antenna ears turning satellite-like hearing voles

Santa Cruz, Sacramento, Point Reyes
       their apex predators mostly wolves,
             mountain lions, or killed by humans
Here, they are thriving, hunting
         blue   eyed   chance mutation

Lucille Lang Day

POETRY AND THE LANGUAGE OF SCIENCE

BEFORE I BECAME A POET, I trained as a scientist, and science has always played an important role in my poetry. I was already using science in my poetry by 1971, when I was a senior in biology at UC Berkeley and wrote a poem called "e–" (the symbol for an electron) about Heisenberg's uncertainty principle. Throughout the 1970s, when I was a graduate student first in zoology and later in science/mathematics education, as well as during the decades that followed, I continued to bring science into my poetry. By doing so, I've made several "discoveries," but I don't mean to imply that these discoveries are unique to me. I believe that others have made these discoveries, too!

My first discovery was that the language of science is beautiful and that it can therefore enhance the beauty of a poem. I don't remember the exact moment I reached this realization, but I definitely knew it in 1979 when I used the words "gallinaceous" and "mycelia" in my poem "Biologist in the Kitchen":

When the tea kettle whistles
I hear a hundred bushtits
emit tandem calls.

Two gallinaceous birds painted on my cup
must be pheasants,
but the coloring is wrong—
too bright for females,
too dull for males.

Sunlight slips easily
under the eaves. Mycelia
bloom by the sink

and when the crickets start to sing
I think of the click and shimmer
of polished bone
in the Vertebrate Museum, intricate
skeletons poised on racks.

I sip my cut black tea,
longing for wind in the forested skull,
where roots embrace whole cities
and fattened ants hang
upside-down, under the grass.

"Gallinaceous" means "pertaining to the Galliformes," an order of heavy-bodied birds that includes pheasants, turkeys, and chickens. "Mycelia" are branching, threadlike masses that connect a fungal or bacterial colony. I had a dirty sink!

Next, I realized that poetry uses all of the same mental skills as science, plus more. Poetry uses logic, reasoning, observation, and knowledge, just like science. Logic in poetry, though, is not necessarily linear, inductive, or deductive. A poem can move by association, and it can move in a circle. It can break up grammar and reshuffle the parts of speech as surely as a chemical reaction breaks up molecules and reshuffles atoms.

Science uses intuition, just like poetry. A famous example is chemist August Kekulé's realization that the benzene molecule must have a ring structure, an idea that came to him after he had a daydream of a snake biting its own tail. Also like poetry, science involves aesthetics: scientists and mathematicians often refer to the "beauty" of an experiment or proof.

In the 1980s and 1990s I became aware of other poets who were using science extensively in their work. Pattiann Rogers, whose first book, *The Expectations of Light*, was published in 1981, thrilled me with the specificity of her descriptions of biological systems and the recognition of human cognition as one component of these systems. In 1994 I read Alison Hawthorne Deming's first book, *Science*, and then in 1998 her second, *The Monarchs: A Poem Sequence*. When I read the poems of Rogers and Deming, I connected with them so deeply that I wished I had written them myself. That being impossible, I contented myself with being inspired by and learning from these poets instead.

Science looks askance at emotional reactions, whereas poetry embraces them, and by doing so, poetry allows a more complete expression of human experience. My poem "Of Light and Love" was sparked by an article that appeared in the *New York Times* on January 18, 2001, and explained that scientists could now bring light to a full stop, hold it, and then send it on its way. The poem is about both love and the science of light:

Forged in the ancient hearts of stars,
it shimmies through space
for eons to illuminate the sea
for the man and woman leaning
into each other at the end of the pier.

The sun floods Earth with it, too—
pure energy filling the sky
like a porcelain bowl
spilling minuscule beads
to bounce off petals, leaves
and the throat of a hummingbird,
into cone cells of my retina,
saying send the message
"like a red, red rose"
to the cortex now.

It's the reason for shadows
of willows dancing in wind
at the edge of a pond
and the product of two
bodies raised to white heat,
daring me to see
"a soul at the white heat."

Streaming from the moon's face,
it reveals two roads converging
in a yellow wood
but conceals the Milky Way.

Two candles beating
like hearts in silver holders
create it from paraffin
and dark air—small
household gods
standing on the buffet.

Crammed with invisible color
or teased into a rainbow
singing in vibrant shades,
it's not time's fool. It always
wins the race, yet slows
to a stop in chilled
rubidium gas, disappears
like a stalled dream
or lost possibility
frozen in space, until
after years of experiments
and wrong calculations
you find warm arms
around you at dawn
and know you're done
running in place.

The next discovery to emerge for me from the process of writing poetry and reading other poets was that poetry could be used as a medium for communicating the ideas of science and deepening our understanding of them. I concluded that poetry could be used routinely in teaching science at every level. As someone who has read both a whole lot of scientific papers and a whole lot of poems, I can tell you that reading the poems has definitely been more fun, so I think that poetry can be used to catalyze students' interest in science.

By allowing the inclusion of emotions, either implicitly or explicitly, I discovered that a science poem can take a political position, and I've especially been drawn to promoting environmental awareness through poetry. My poem "Global Warming in the Galápagos," which appears in my book *Birds of San Pancho and Other Poems of Place* (2020), contains images showing the effects of climate change on flora and fauna of the Galápagos Islands:

Three years without rain,
and incense trees are gray, leafless
in what should be the wet season.

Without the trees, where will red-
footed boobies with blue beaks
build nests where fluffy chicks can hatch?

Even prickly pear cacti, looking so much
like clusters of spiny ping pong paddles,
are turning brown and dying.

What will happen to iguanas that eat
the cacti, and lava lizards that nibble
lice from the iguanas' necks and backs?

A warming sea also brings El Niño
with too much rain, flooding,
overheated currents where penguins

can't find fish, and beaches so hot
that green turtle eggs can't hatch.
When iguanas can no longer regulate

their body temperature, giant tortoises
and blue-footed boobies will gather
like refugees and strike out for cooler land.

I have not, to the best of my knowledge, made any true scientific pre-discoveries, as Poe, Whitman, and Stein did. However, through poetry I have come to scientific insights that I had not previously read elsewhere. One of these was the realization that the extinction of species and the extinction of languages are linked. My understanding of this connection grew out of writing my poem "Lost Languages" in 2016:

It isn't just Hittite, Trojan and Sumerian,
or even Mohegan, Yana and Natchez,
all long gone, but also the hundreds
that have slipped away since 1950,
while the last Madeiran Large White butterfly
flickered among the trees of the laurisilva,
the last West African black rhino
ran across the savannah, chased by poachers
after its horn, coveted as an aphrodisiac in China,
and the last Javan tiger, stripes rippling,
was poisoned, its forest habitat cleared for rice.

Lucille Roubedeaux, last surviving speaker
of the Osage language in Oklahoma,
died in 2005; Marie Smith Jones,
last speaker of Eyak, died in Alaska in 2008.

Biologists say ninety-nine point nine percent
of all species that ever existed are now extinct.
Perhaps the same is true of languages.
Who knows what Cro-Magnons said
to one another in sickness, love or fear?
Now so many ways of dreaming and perceiving
are disappearing, but as Mojave, Comanche,
Bolo and Beezen slip away, so do salmon,
salamanders, rainforests and redwoods,
and even the speakers of English, Russian
and Chinese become one with the red wolf,
mongoose, numbat and tarsier in their fate.

I now know that others have thought of this too: the same forces of capitalism, habitat destruction, and globalization that drive the loss of species also lead to the loss of languages.

I'll conclude with a quote from *Braiding Sweetgrass* (2013), by Robin Wall Kimmerer. In describing the language of science, she says, "But beneath the richness of its vocabulary and its descriptive power, something is missing, the same something that swells around you and in you when you listen to the world." Kimmerer, a botanist and a member of the Citizen Potawatomi Nation, was making the point that this "something missing" can be found in Indigenous languages. I will add that it can also be found in poetry.

❦ ❦ ❦

₳BOUT THE ₵ONTRIBUTORS

ELIZABETH BRADFIELD is the author of *Toward Antarctica, Once Removed, Approaching Ice*, and *Interpretive Work*, as well as *Theorem*, a collaboration with artist Antonia Contro. Bradfied's work has been published in the *New Yorker, Atlantic Monthly, West Branch, Poetry, Orion*, the *Kenyon Review*, and elsewhere, and her honors include the Audre Lorde Award from the Publishing Triangle, the James Laughlin Award from the Academy of American Poets, a Bread Loaf scholarship, and a Stegner Fellowship. For the past twenty-some years, she has worked as a naturalist and guide locally and abroad. Editor-in-chief of Broadsided Press and a contributing editor at the *Alaska Quarterly Review*, she lives on Cape Cod and teaches creative writing at Brandeis University.
https://www.ebradfield.com

LUCILLE LANG DAY is the author of seven full-length poetry collections and four poetry chapbooks. Her latest collection is *Birds of San Pancho and Other Poems of Place*. She has also coedited two anthologies—*Fire and Rain: Ecopoetry of California* and *Red Indian Road West: Native American Poetry from California*—and published two children's books and a memoir, *Married at Fourteen: A True Story*. Her many honors include the Blue Light Poetry Prize, two PEN Oakland–Josephine Miles Literary Awards, the Joseph Henry Jackson Award, and eleven Pushcart Prize nominations. The founder and publisher of a small press, Scarlet Tanager Books, she received her MA in English and MFA in creative writing at San Francisco State University, and her BA in biological sciences, MA in zoology, and PhD in science/mathematics education at the University of California, Berkeley. She lives in Oakland, California.
https://lucillelangday.com

ALISON HAWTHORNE DEMING'S most recent books include the poetry collection *Stairway to Heaven* and *Death Valley: Painted Light*, a collaboration with photographer Stephen E. Strom. Her essay collection *Zoologies: On Animals and the Human Spirit* was published by Milkweed Editions in 2014. A recent Guggenheim Fellow, she is the author of *Science and Other Poems*, winner of the Walt Whitman Award of the Academy of American Poets; *The Monarchs: A Poem Sequence; Genius Loci; Rope*; and three nonfiction books, *Temporary Homelands, Writing the Sacred Into the Real*, and *The Edges of the Civilized World*, a finalist for the PEN Center West Award. She edited *Poetry of the American West: A Columbia Anthology* and coedited with Lauret E. Savoy *The Colors of Nature: Essays on Culture, Identity, and the Natural World*. She is Regents Professor at the University of Arizona. Her new nonfiction book, *A Woven World*, came out from Counterpoint Press in August 2021.
https://alisonhawthornedeming.com

ANN FISHER-WIRTH'S sixth book of poems is *The Bones of Winter Birds*. Her fifth book, *Mississippi*, is a poetry/photography collaboration with the photographer Maude Schuyler Clay. With Laura-Gray Street, Fisher-Wirth coedited *The Ecopoetry Anthology*. She is a senior fellow of the Black Earth Institute; has had residencies at the Mesa Refuge, Djerassi, Hedgebrook, and CAMAC, in France; and has received numerous awards for her work, including a Mississippi Institute of Arts and Letters Poetry Award, two Mississippi Arts Council Poetry Fellowships, a *Malahat Review* Long Poem Prize, a Rita Dove Poetry Award, and fifteen Pushcart nominations. Fisher-Wirth was a 2017 Poet in Residence at Randolph College in Virginia, and she has received senior Fulbright Scholar awards to Switzerland and Sweden. She is a professor of English and directs the Environmental Studies program at the University of Mississippi. https://annfisherwirth.com

ALLISON ADELLE HEDGE COKE'S books include *Burn, Streaming, Blood Run, Off-Season City Pipe, Dog Road Woman, Sing: Poetry from the Indigenous Americas, Effigies I, II,* and *III,* and *Rock, Ghost, Willow, Deer: A Story of Survival*. Her awards include an American Book Award, a King-Chávez-Parks Award, a PEN Southwest Book Award, a 2016 Library of Congress Witter Bynner Fellowship, a 2021 George Garrett Award, and induction into the Texas Institute of Letters in 2021. She is founding faculty of the MFA in Writing and Publishing program at the Vermont College of Fine Arts, as well as a Distinguished Professor of Creative Writing at the University of California, Riverside. Hedge Coke is of mixed heritage and was raised in North Carolina, Canada, and on the Great Plains. She directs the Lit Sandhill CraneFest and is working in film. https://profiles.ucr.edu/app/home/profile/allisonh

Selected Works by the Contributors

BRADFIELD, ELIZABETH

Theorem. Portland, OR: Poetry Northwest Editions, 2020.

Toward Antarctica. Pasadena, CA: Boreal Books/Red Hen Press, 2019.

Once Removed. New York: Persea Books, 2015.

Approaching Ice. New York: Persea Books, 2010.

Interpretive Work. Pasadena, CA: Arktoi Books/Red Hen Press, 2008.

DAY, LUCILLE LANG

Birds of San Pancho and Other Poems of Place. San Francisco, CA: Blue Light Press, 2020.

Fire and Rain: Ecopoetry of California. Coedited with Ruth Nolan. Oakland, CA: Scarlet Tanager Books, 2018.

"Poet as Scientist." In *Waccamaw: a journal of contemporary literature*, no. 13, fall 2014.

"Rhymes with Reason: Poetry, Science, the Planet, and the Mind." In *Redwood Coast Review*, fall 2014.

The Curvature of Blue. West Somerville, MA: Červená Barva Press, 2009.

The Book of Answers. Georgetown, KY: Finishing Line Press, 2006.

Infinities. Mena, AR: Cedar Hill Publications, 2002.

Self-Portrait with Hand Microscope. Berkeley, CA: Berkeley Poets' Workshop and Press, 1982. Winner of the Joseph Henry Jackson Award from the San Francisco Foundation.

DEMING, ALISON HAWTHORNE

Stairway to Heaven. New York: Penguin, 2016.

Death Valley: Painted Light. With photographer Stephen E. Strom. Staunton, VA: George F. Thompson Publishing, 2016.

Rope. New York: Penguin, 2009.

Genius Loci. New York: Penguin, 2005.

"Poetry and Science: A View from the Divide." In *Creative Nonfiction*, no. 11, 1998. Winner of *Creative Nonfiction's* Bayer Award in Science Writing..

The Monarchs: A Poem Sequence. Baton Rouge, LA: Louisiana State University Press, 1997.

Science and Other Poems. Baton Rouge, LA: Louisiana State University Press, 1994. Winner of the Walt Whitman Award from the Academy of American Poets.

FISHER-WIRTH, ANN

The Bones of Winter Birds. West Caldwell, NJ: Terrapin Books, 2019.

Mississippi. With photography by Maude Schuyler Clay. San Antonio, TX: Wings Press, 2018.

The Ecopoetry Anthology. Coedited with Laura-Gray Street. San Antonio, TX: Trinity University Press, 2013; third printing 2020.

Dream Cabinet. San Antonio, TX: Wings Press, 2012.

HEDGE COKE, ALLISON ADELLE

Look at This Blue. Minneapolis, MN: Coffee House Press, forthcoming, March 2022.

Effigies III. Coedited with Brandi Nalani McDougall and Craig Santos Perez. UK: Salt Publishing, 2019. A collection of four debut books by queer Pacific Islander women poets.

Burn. Illustrated by Dustin Illetwahke Mater. Cheshire, MA: MadHat Press, 2017.

Effigies II (editor). UK: Salt Publishing, 2019. A collection of five debut books by Native women poets from the U.S. mainland.

Streaming. Minneapolis, MN: Coffee House Press, 2014; album, Long Person Records (Yvwi Gvnahita), 2014.

Sing: Poetry from the Indigenous Americas (editor). Tucson, AZ: University of Arizona Press, 2011.

Effigies (editor). UK: Salt Publishing, 2009. A collection of four debut books by Native women poets from the Pacific Rim.

Blood Run. UK: Salt Publishing, 2006; released in the United States in 2007.

Off-Season City Pipe. Minneapolis, MN: Coffee House Press, 2005.

Dog Road Woman. Minneapolis, MN: Coffee House Press, 1997.

References

BRADFIELD, ELIZABETH

Gumbs, Alexis Pauline. *Undrowned: Black Feminist Lessons from Marine Mammals*. Chico, CA: AK Press, 2020.

Kimmerer, Robin Wall. *Gathering Moss*. Corvallis, OR: Oregon State University Press, 2003.

Nelson, Richard. *The Island Within*. New York: North Point Press, 1989, and Vintage Books Edition, a division of Random House, 1991.

Saulitis, Eva. *Into Great Silence*. Boston, MA: Beacon Press, 2013.

Saulitis, Eva. *Leaving Resurrection: Chronicles of a Whale Scientist*. Boreal Books: Fairbanks, AK, 2008.

DAY, LUCILLE LANG

Kimmerer, Robin Wall. *Braiding Sweetgrass*. Minneapolis, MN: Milkweed Editions, 2013.

Lehrer, Jonah. *Proust Was a Neuroscientist*. New York: Houghton Mifflin, 2007.

Poe, Edgar Allan. *Eureka: A Prose Poem*. 1848.

Rogers, Pattiann. *The Expectations of Light*. Princeton, NJ: Princeton University Press, 1981.

DEMING, ALISON HAWTHORNE

Ammons, A. R. *Garbage: A Poem*. New York: Norton, 2002, first published in 1993.

Gay, Ross. *Catalog of Unabashed Gratitude*. Pittsburgh, PA: University of Pittsburgh Press, 2015.

Hahn, Kimiko. *Toxic Flora*. New York: Norton, 2010.

McKibben, Bill. *Falter: Has the Human Game Begun to Play Itself Out?* New York: Holt Paperbacks, 2020.

Wright, C. D. *Casting Deep Shade*. Port Townsend, WA: Copper Canyon Press, 2019.

FISHER-WIRTH, ANN

Carson, Rachel. *Silent Spring*. New York: Houghton Mifflin, 1962.

Haskell, David George. *The Forest Unseen: A Year's Watch in Nature*. New York: Penguin, 2013.

Kolbert, Elizabeth. *The Sixth Extinction: An Unnatural History*. New York: Picador, 2015.

Lanham, J. Drew. *The Home Place: Memoirs of a Colored Man's Love Affair with Nature*. Minneapolis, MN: Milkweed Editions, 2017.

Magdoff, Fred, and Foster, John Bellamy. *What Every Environmentalist Needs to Know about Capitalism*. New York: Monthly Review Press, 2011.

Ray, Janisse. *Ecology of a Cracker Childhood*. Minneapolis, MN: Milkweed Editions, 2015, first published in 1999.

Sheldrake, Merlin. *Entangled Life: How Fungi Make Our Worlds, Change Our Minds, and Shape Our Futures*. New York: Random House, 2021.

Smart, Christopher. "Jubilate Agno." Eighteenth century, first published in 1939.

Williams, William Carlos. *Kora in Hell*. San Francisco: City Lights Books, 1969, first published in 1920.

Williams, William Carlos. *Spring and All*. Cambridge, MA: New Directions, 2011, first published in 1923.

HEDGE COKE, ALLISON ADELLE
Sze, Arthur. *The Glass Constellation: New and Collected Poems*. Port Townsend, WA: Copper Canyon Press, 2021.

Sze, Arthur. *Sight Lines*. Port Townsend, WA: Copper Canyon Press, 2019.

$\mathcal{A}$CKNOWLEDGMENTS

Many thanks to Allison Adelle Hedge Coke for proposing *Poetry and Science* when the contributors and I served on a panel of the same title at the AWP (Association of Writers and Writing Programs) annual conference in March 2021. — L. L. D.

Unless otherwise specified, all poems and quotations are reprinted with permission of their authors.

Bradfield, Elizabeth. "Misapprehensions of Nature," "We All Want to See a Mammal," and "Right Whale: Death as Spectacle" are from *Once Removed*, Persea Books, 2015. "Permeable" was published in the *Kenyon Review*.

Day, Lucille Lang. "Biologist in the Kitchen" is from *Self-Portrait with Hand Microscope*, Berkeley Poets' Workshop and Press, 1982. "Of Light and Love" is from *Infinities*, Cedar Hill Publications, 2002. "Global Warming in the Galápagos" is from *Birds of San Pancho and Other Poems of Place*, Blue Light Press, 2020. "Lost Languages" was published in *Psychological Perspectives*.

Deming, Alison Hawthorne. "Letter to 2050" was published in *Scientific American* in January 2021. "Science" is from *Science and Other Poems*, Louisiana State University Press, 1994. Copyright © 1994 by Alison Hawthorne Deming. Reprinted by permission of Louisiana State University Press. "1," "18," and "22" are from *The Monarchs: A Poem Sequence*, Louisiana State University Press, 1998.

Fisher-Wirth, Ann. "Winter Day on the Whirlpool Trails" and "Catalpa" were published in *Mantis*. "Val Corsaglia" was published in *Prairie Schooner*. "Credo" is from *Dream Cabinet*, Wings Press, 2012.

Hedge Coke, Allison Adelle. "Waiting for the Last Lunar Eclipse, 2004" is from *Off-Season City Pipe*, Coffee House Press, 2005. "Blue Whale," "bluecurls," and "Chance Mutation" are from *Look at This Blue*, Coffee House Press, forthcoming, March 2022.

Nelson, Richard. Quotation is from *The Island Within*, North Point Press, 1989. Copyright © 1989 by Richard Nelson. Published by Vintage Books Edition, 1991. Reprinted by permission of the Estate of Richard Nelson.

Saulitis, Eva. Quotations are from *Leaving Resurrection: Chronicles of a Whale Scientist*, Boreal Books, 2008. Copyright © 2008 by Eva Saulitis. Reprinted by permission of Red Hen Press, Pasadena, CA.

Sze, Arthur. "Net Light" is from *Sight Lines*, Copper Canyon Press, 2019, and *The Glass Constellation: New and Collected Poems*, Copper Canyon Press, 2021.

Williams, William Carlos. "Spring and All" is from *Spring and All* (1923), which is in the public domain.

Also from Scarlet Tanager Books

Bone Strings by Anne Coray
poetry, 80 pages

Fire and Rain: Ecopoetry of California
edited by Lucille Lang Day and Ruth Nolan
poetry, 462 pages

The Rainbow Zoo by Lucille Lang Day
illustrated by Gina Aoay Orosco
children's book, 26 pages

Wild One by Lucille Lang Day
poetry, 100 pages

The "Fallen Western Star" Wars: A Debate About Literary California
edited by Jack Foley
essays, 88 pages

Catching the Bullet and Other Stories by Daniel Hawkes
fiction, 64 pages

Luck by Marc Elihu Hofstadter
poetry, 104 pages

Visions: Paintings Seen Through the Optic of Poetry
by Marc Elihu Hofstadter
poetry, 72 pages

Embrace by Risa Kaparo
poetry, 70 pages

Catch and Other Poems by Richard Michael Levine
poetry, 82 pages

crimes of the dreamer by Naomi Ruth Lowinsky
poetry, 82 pages

red clay is talking by Naomi Ruth Lowinsky
poetry, 142 pages

The Number Before Infinity by Zack Rogow
poetry, 72 pages

Red Indian Road West: Native American Poetry from California
edited by Kurt Schweigman and Lucille Lang Day
poetry, 110 pages

The Book of Geezer by John Teton
fiction, 268 pages

Call Home by Judy Wells
poetry, 92 pages

Everything Irish by Judy Wells
poetry, 112 pages

*Turning a Train of Thought Upside Down:
An Anthology of Women's Poetry*
edited by Andrena Zawinksi
poetry, 100 pages

Scarlet Tanager
BOOKS

POETRY & SCIENCE

CPSIA information can be obtained
at www.ICGtesting.com
Printed in the USA
FSHW010723201021
85555FS